C000176262

Shield
Jamie Hale

VERVE
POETRY PRESS
BIRMINGHAM

PUBLISHED BY VERVE POETRY PRESS
https://vervepoetrypress.com
mail@vervepoetrypress.com

FIRST PUBLISHED JAN 2021
REPRINTED JAN 2021

Printed and bound in the UK
by Positive Print, Birmingham

ISBN: 978-1-912565-49-8

CONTENTS

crying silently and telling him this   6

our quiet moments at home at night   7

a year away from now, i promise, is a shield   8

not ever short of your love for me   9

i see their eyes and figures in my sleep   10

my fears, i wait; i receive no reply   11

we don't talk about anything left unsaid   12

and urns they say that we were the victors   13

like this; all legs and lungs and eyes and death   14

the pandemic has made monsters of us all   15

a marble, sent skittering across the floor   16

they'll save anyone before you   17

give me more than charity to live   18

do i live so much less a life than her?   19

the doctors never entered with good news   20

they died of a disease that was maybe treatable   21

or this is all a dream just a fever dream   22

the final, beautiful, honest word   23

if you can it's such a bad time to die   24

we can tell ourselves all is well   25

say the epidemic gave them, at least, a fighting chance   26

Acknowledgements

*For Ismail Mohamed Abdulwahab
and everyone who died in the
COVID-19 pandemic*

Shield

i

i write an email to my GP telling him please
i love my life telling him please i want to be
the opposite of a Do Not Resuscitate order
the opposite of a patient you'd give a quiet death

o god let me die loudly let my ribs crack
i will arc with shock please i'd rather die
as i've lived as i've lived filled with love and
i'd rather die fierce as myself, every time

every bloody time. so i tell him what i do
wave my accomplishments my desperate
shield of fragile silk; i hide and tell him
i have value over and over and over

and over as if i wasn't sat at the keys
crying silently and telling him this

ii

we are cleaning our hands
together; steady; when i touch
your once soft skin it cracks
turns to rough sand

your love for me is peeling
off in shards of crumbling skin
and i am awed, in this season
of epidemic we have each other

the dog. the newly sorted cupboards
enough food, the frantic spring clean
the washing of door handles
over and over and over and still

keep us breathing like this, together
our quiet moments at home at night

iii

it is confirmed that i am not a priority
for treatment my doctor delicately said
that it would be saved for people who
would survive. my ventilator stares

at me i stare at myself and out of the window
at the sky but the virus is staring back
from beneath your skin you have become
a timebomb turning me in bed a timebomb

emptying my catheter a timebomb
my trust in your precautions is not a shield
if you come to explode is not a shield
if i catch it from you is not a shield

i stare at the future feel it staring back
a year away from now, i promise, is a shield

iv

hanging gel from door handles
on ribbons. fuck christmas we won't
make it that far if we do let's cheer
whip it down drink as bitter booze

gently kiss your elderly aunt
wildly kiss your shining urn promise it
a better funeral next year promise
yourself next time you'll be ready

not caught short of alcohol hand gel
short of gloves short as newly-shorn
hair short of everything and no hand
to hold but stuttering screens

and somehow still not short of you
not ever short of your love for me

v

we haven't had a day off since this
started not that we know when the
dying started but we're not touching
patients just crunching figures seeking

patterns but nothing comes not even
a day to rest i thought i was done with
migraines but this stress. if there is
no vaccine i will not look myself

in the eye ever again. i will not think
the damned can be saved i will not
believe in medicine i'm done with
the dead being numbers just numbers

on a screen numbers staring at me
i see their eyes and figures in my sleep

vi

my doctor writes back he says
i am stuck between a rock
and a hard place i swallow
the cliché the bitter cliché

the things that make me vulnerable.
i am not a good candidate intensive
care is saved for where it would
work his email fragmenting, my

body falling into fragments, the
fragment that works, the fragment
that damns me, the fragment that
will be will not be do not no please

always resuscitate me i send him back
my fears, i wait; i receive no reply

vii

i call my parents we don't talk
about anything unsaid we just
talk silently about nothing together
i don't want to engage with this

it's not like i have brought it up
how do you say if i don't survive
this, this is what i want. the notes
are on my computer anyway i tell

people my wishes that way.
it won't matter to me if they
don't listen i try to talk to everyone
i choke on words like coiled rope

down my throat i call my parents
we don't talk about anything we left unsaid

viii

the war had ended and we, the survivors
all rotten-toed and trench-tired went home safe
to the Kansas base and we had survived the war
survived the sinking mud and shells and

just when we thought the war had ended safe
and heading back home from Kansas sick, a cough
of relief we said we spread across the states
to the arms of our families coughing a bit

but just a bit we said and not that bad and then
we were dying they were dying dying and nobody
knew the flu had dogged our footsteps home
all those hungry ghosts still out there entrenched

and they say that we were the victors in coffins
and urns they say that we were the victors

ix

am i hysterical i think i can see bugs
everywhere crawling wash your hands
please, please i beg you, please
PLEASE wash your goddamn hands

and now get the blood off them
no get the blood off both of us
no i know i can see you i can't breathe
that damning spot of filth

they talked about cocooning people
like me and that is a smothering cloth
late at night i walk the streets in my head
pacing and pacing and pacing for air

bugs are crawling on your skin and i also crawl
like this; all legs and lungs and eyes and death

x

i'm thinking of ismail abdulwahab today.
i remember how it felt to nearly die
the sky closing in how i held onto her hand
and felt the luckiest person alive

i'm thinking of loneliness. that long
night's wait for her to come. remembering
what it was to be thirteen and on the
brink of something big. about to become.

thinking of the line between bravado
and need. the desire to be someone. theft
and life. the prices we pay. ask others
to pay. thinking of death and burial alone

we are far too young to know the world
the pandemic has made monsters of us all

xi

if i lie just right in bed a strip of blue cuts
round the edge of my window frame i
can see the sky. i'm reminded it's bigger
than you and me the sky is bigger than our

terror she sings to herself. the sky
does not see the mess we've made
she just drinks and sobs out the needed rain
so we ignore her plaintive cries. the sky

is bigger than i thought it was after so long
indoors. bigger than majesty and striking
our beauty with thunderbolts
it's as if i thought the world had shrunk

and was sitting in my palms, and then
a marble, sent skittering across the floor

xii

my ventilator is set to 14 and 5
these are normal he says i type it frantic
he's still a child in my head my brother says
don't let your oxygen levels drop

below 80 don't increase your
ventilator settings too much you'd risk
gastric insufflation remember
tidal volume is estimated based on

what's left in the lung as it closes
remember love is based on tides
as they come in closer remember
to bring your own ventilator

remember if they're overwhelmed
they'll save anyone before you

xiii

i wrote another letter today the ward
is running out of masks i saw nurses
using them for days at a time there was
no answer and now sister is sick

her children have gone to their
father hopefully they're not infected
how is this not my fault? how have i
not failed my colleagues? i wrote a

letter today there was no answer but
some costume designers delivered
handmade scrubs i almost cried is this
what we're reduced to desperate gifts

i'll do anything to survive but please
give me more than charity to live

xiv

they're rationing air now
have a ventilator. don't. have it taken away
too slow to recover. the fastest survive
there is no way out any more.

a hospital almost ran out of air.
a dependent patient has their ventilator
taken, dies so someone else
can recover a little faster yet

i cling to mine train my carers
to change settings i make
them promise to breathe for me
with a bag of air when nobody else will

i look at my love in the next room.
do i live so much less a life than her?

xv

my father is at home like me we talk
on the phone sometimes, my brother
is a paramedic, my mother is trying
to hold it all together, my wife is afraid

of going out in case she brings it home
and the dog is bored and sleeps all the time
another summer is coming and again
i am indoors, malnourished, another sore

history repeating as farce the pale
horse the paler rider the pain of fear the
shame the blame the last time this
story was told it ended the same way with

me safe in your arms in a hospital bed
the doctors never entered with good news

xvi

the spanish army found pensioners dead
in care home beds near madrid after
the carers had fled. there will be a trial
of the carers they were 'absolutely

abandoned' these people in care homes dying
of something were murdered and i
could have been one of them they
who grew up in a state apparently valuing

life above all else. how long were they
alone i want to beg for never i know
it feels like forever so now is not
the time for my questions of politics now is not

the time to ask about complicity when
they died of a disease that was maybe treatable

xvii

every day something new comes online
today i ate garlic out of the bulb and
my breath scored the air and i felt alive
but if it shortens the length of winter colds

then that way lies the madness of fantasy
cures. i take vitamin d but i was always meant to.
who needs the sun when pills provide it.
soften the sharp corners of these walls.

it's bleach to kill the bugs, or breathing
if i wear a mask can i go outside? still no
that way lies the madness of hospital-white paint
i dream i catch coronavirus and somehow survive

more likely an early death than simple immunity
or this is all a dream just a fever dream

xviii

i'm tired of writing headlines tired
of counting the death toll my eyes
are full of emails "they let my father
die why did they not save him was

he not enough and i...". i'm tired of writing
headlines it's enough to try to
save them once. this is not an essential
service but i'm still writing headlines

sometimes i dream that someone sees
the poetry in these stark words and draws it out
says to me my comments are tender stories
but please let's make this art take these ghosts

let someone else give them
the final, beautiful, honest word

xix

they cancelled all the funerals
you know it's immediate family
only right? this is a bad time to
die if you wanted that party

the patients never listen i come
in after they no longer listen
i hear their dreams in crumpled
pockets in engagement rings

still boxed. they cancelled
all the funerals now we have them
alone and nobody lays their ghosts
to rest without a party

maybe you should wait a few months
if you can it's such a bad time to die

xx

it's dying down. by which i mean
the dying itself is fading by which
we mean more people die every day
but a fewer more and that's better

isn't it? pandemic makes epidemiologists
of us all and the data swims in front
of my eyes like the sun on hot tarmac
in the hills of mallorca where i once

sort of lived. the outside world is dangerous
and unreal all the same. it's been three
months the sky is an illusion and air
a fantasy i write to you from delirium

but in this little space alone together
we can tell ourselves all is well

xxi

if i die dump a fucking urn of ash
and bone outside parliament lie
say it was me tell them i dreamed of
a life that their decisions killed me

if i die don't say i had nothing better to offer
no answer only harping from a distance
making selfish arguments as if to say
'when you choose who to save, choose me'

if i die take my ashes and put a pinch
in each envelope of flower seed favours
left after our wedding send them to friends
think of the seeds Ed planted in Lombardy

growing wild and weedy under lockdown
say the epidemic gave them, at least, a fighting chance

ACKNOWLEDGEMENTS

This pamphlet could not have existed without the support and encouragement of so many people – and as with all acknowledgements I will have forgotten countless significant influences.

In the poetry world, my thanks go to Ruth Harrison, Bobby Nayer, and the Spread the Word team, as well as the other London Writers Awards for Poetry winners of 2018 for their critical feedback on my earlier work, and to Mona Arshi for her feedback and guidance. Crucial appreciation goes to Nathalie Teitler and Mimi Khalvati, whose generous support, suggestions, and editing have made this pamphlet what it is, and to Stuart Bartholomew and Verve for publishing it.

In other areas, thanks to the Barbican team, especially Toni Racklin, Angie Smith, Alex Jamieson, and Bernie Whittle for all their support with my creative work, to Charlie Covell and the KAOS crew for believing in and pushing me and my writing, and to Nigel Lester for his mentoring.

I also want to thank Dr F, J&J, my team of support workers and all the health and other professionals out there keeping me alive and well.

Personal thanks go to my family, especially my grandmothers, who both loved poetry, my grandfather, who has always supported me in all my endeavours, my parents, and my brother. They also go to CN Lester for being there to support and encourage me from the start, in every single way.

Most of all, thanks go to my beloved wife, Emily Robinson, to whom this pamphlet is an extended love letter.

ABOUT THE AUTHOR:

Jamie Hale is a poet and essayist based in South-East London. Their solo show, NOT DYING, has been performed at the Lyric Theatre in Hammersmith and at CRIPtic - their showcase at the Barbican Centre. They have had poetry published in *Magma*, *Rialto*, and *Poetry Quarterly*. They are currently working on a major screenwriting project. In 2018 they won one of the London Writers' Awards for Poetry, and in 2019 they were shortlisted for the Jerwood Fellowships. *Shield* is their first poetry publication.

ABOUT VERVE POETRY PRESS

Verve Poetry Press is a fairly new and already award-winning press focussing hard on meeting a need in Birmingham - a need for the vibrant poetry scene here in Brum to find a way to present itself to the poetry world via publication. Co-founded by Stuart Bartholomew and Amerah Saleh, it is publishing poets from all corners of the city - poets that represent the city's varied and energetic qualities and will communicate its many poetic stories.

Added to this is a colourful pamphlet series featuring poets who have previously performed at our sister festival - and a poetry show series which captures the magic of longer poetry performance pieces by poets such as Polarbear and Matt Abbott.

In 2019 the press was voted Most Innovative Publisher at the Saboteur Awards, and won the Publisher's Award for Poetry Pamphlets at the Michael Marks Awards.

Like the festival, we will strive to think about poetry in inclusive ways and embrace the multiplicity of approaches towards this glorious art.

www.vervepoetrypress.com
@VervePoetryPres
mail@vervepoetrypress.com